# DK Watch me grow

# Kitten

# DK

LONDON, NEW YORK, MUNICH,
MELBOURNE and DELHI

Written and edited by Lisa Magloff
Designed by Sonia Moore and Mary Sandberg
Publishing Manager  Sue Leonard
Managing Art Editor  Clare Shedden
Jacket Design  Tony Chung
Picture Researcher  Liz Moore
Production  Shivani Pandey
DTP Designer  Almudena Díaz

First published in Great Britain in 2005 by
Dorling Kindersley Limited
80 Strand, London WC2R 0RL

A Penguin Company

Copyright © 2005 Dorling Kindersley Limited, London

A CIP catalogue record for this book
is available from the British Library.

ISBN 1-4053-0845-1

Colour reproduction by Media, Development and Printing, Ltd.
Printed and bound by South China Printing Co, Ltd., China

see our complete catalogue at

www.dk.com

# Contents

# I'm a cat

I can live almost anywhere. I have soft fur to keep me warm and protect me. I love to scamper, play, and hunt for mice.

A long, bendy tail helps a cat to balance.

Sharp claws help cats to hunt and to grab things.

Here are Mum and Dad with all our friends and family.

Cats' eyes can see well in the dark.

**Lullaby cat**
Cats spend most of the day sleeping. They can sleep just about any time, and in any position.

Whiskers also help cats to balance.

Now turn the page and watch us grow.....

# My Mum and Dad

My Mum and Dad live next door to each other. They met in the garden. Dad had to chase away a lot of other males before he had kittens with Mum.

**Keeping clean**
Cats love to keep their fur clean and neat. Dad washes himself by licking his paws and then rubbing his face.

This mother cat's tummy is very big because it is almost time for her litter of kittens to be born.

This is my Mum..... and this is my Dad!

# I'm one day old

I'm hungry. It's time for me to nurse. Mum helps us all to find her milk by gently pushing us with her paws. It's a big squeeze but we all fit in.

The mother cat lies quietly while her litter drinks.

## Newborns
For the first few days, the kittens spend almost all of their time lying together in a pile, keeping warm.

# Kitten facts

. . . . . . . . . . . . . . . . . . . . .

🐈 The kittens can't see, but they can smell where Mum is.

🐈 Newborn kittens sleep most of the time.

🐈 During feeding, the kittens will purr if they are getting enough milk.

# Mum washes us

We are too little to wash ourselves,
so Mum does it by licking us all over.
This not only keeps our fur clean,
it also makes us feel safe and happy.

### A free ride

Baby kittens can't walk,
so when Mum wants to
move them, she picks them
up gently in her mouth.
They hold still and tuck
up their legs.

It's my sister's turn to be cleaned.

# I'm two weeks old

At last! My eyes are open so I can finally see where I am going. Now I can start to practice wobbly walking. I can also hear much better than I could when I was born.

Great! Now I can see my brothers and sisters!

## Night sight

When they are grown up these kittens will see better at night than we can. They will use this super vision to hunt at night.

This little kitten is learning to stand up.

The kittens call to Mum so she always knows where they are.

# Now I can play

I'm four weeks old and full of energy.
My brothers and sisters and I love to play.
We learn to pounce by practicing on Mum's
tail, but I don't think she likes it very much.

**Ready, steady, go!**
Kittens will play
with almost
anything that
moves. This is
how they learn
to hunt.

Mum's tail makes a
handy toy for the kittens.

## Lunch bunch

The kittens are still nursing,
but they are also starting
to eat solid food.

I think it's time for you to play outside...

# Play fighting

My brother and I pretend to fight with each other. It's just a game, and no one gets hurt.

I hide in the grass and wait to pounce.

The kitten's tail helps her to balance while she leaps.

This is just play, so the kittens don't use their claws.

## Scaredy cat

This kitten has never seen a frog before. He is scared, so he is puffing himself up and trying to look bigger.

# Let's explore

We are ten weeks old and
are very curious. This branch
is a fun place to explore.
Climbing up was easy,
but it will be harder to
climb down.

Is this the way down?

Look at me now. I'm 12 weeks old and very grown up.

**Head over heels**
Cats almost always land on their feet. This is because they can turn around in the air.

# The circle of life goes round and round

Now you know how I turned into a grown-up cat.

# My friends from around the world

Siamese cats love to talk and will meow all day long.

The Red Persian cat has long, silky hair in a solid rusty colour.

Can you see why I am called

The Mackerel Tabby Oriental loves to cuddle and sit on laps.

My cat friends from around the world come in lots of different colours and sizes.

Sphynx cats have short, fine "peach-fuzz" instead of hair.

Manx cats come in many colours, but do not have a tail.

a Blue Shorthair cat?

I'm a Dilute

Calico cat

## Kitten facts

• • • • • • • • • • • • • • • • • • • • • •

🐈 Cats smell with a special organ on the roof of their mouth.

🐈 Cats step with both left legs, then both right legs when they walk or run.

🐈 Cats spend one-third of their time grooming their fur.

# Glossary

## Fur
The thick coat of hair that covers and protects a cat.

## Pounce
To leap or jump on an object or another animal, like a mouse.

## Litter
A group of kittens that are all born at the same time.

## Purr
The noise a cat makes when it is happy and full of food.

## Nurse
When kittens drink milk from their mother's breast.

## Tongue
Cats' tongues are very rough, so they can use them to lick.

## Acknowledgments
The publisher would like to thank the following for their kind permission to reproduce their photographs:
(Key: a=above; c=centre; b=below; l=left; r=right; t=top)
1 Powerstock: Frank Lukasseck c. 2-3 Zefa Visual Media: Frank Lukasseck. 3 Powerstock: Martin Rugner c. 4 Getty Images: Taxi cfl. 4-5 Steven Moore Photography. 4-5 Warren Photographic: Jane Burton x2. 5 Corbis: Helen King cl. 5 Getty Images: Stone tc; Taxi cra. 6 DK Images: Dave King cbl. 6 Steven Moore Photography: cl. 6-7 Steven Moore Photography. 7 DK Images: Jane Burton l, r. 8 DK Images: Jane Burton, bcl. 8-9 DK Images: Jane Burton. 8-9 Steven Moore Photography. 10 OSF/photolibrary.com: IPS Photo Index cb. 10 Warren Photographic: Jane Burton bcr. 11 Warren Photographic: Jane Burton c. 12 Warren Photographic: Jane Burton, cbl. 12-13 Steven Moore Photography. 12-13 Warren Photographic: Jane Burton. 13 Nature Picture Library Ltd: Pete Oxford tl. 14 Warren Photographic: Jane Burton cbr. 14-15 Steven Moore Photography. 14-15 Warren Photographic: Jane Burton.

15 Steven Moore Photography: tl. 15 Warren Photographic: Jane Burton tl. 16 Powerstock: age fotostock cla. 16-17 Powerstock: Martin Rugner/age fotostock. 17 DK Images: Geoff Brightling bc. 17 Steven Moore Photography: bcr. 17 Warren Photographic: Jane Burton br. 18-19 Warren Photographic: Jane Burton. 19 N.H.P.A.: Agence Nature r. 19 Warren Photographic: Jane Burton bl. 20 Alamy Images: Isobel Flynn c. 20 Warren Photographic: Jane Burton cla, ca, cra, crb, bc, bcl, bcr, car, cfl, cfr. 21 OSF/photolibrary.com: Dave Kingdon/IndexStock t. 21 Warren Photographic: Jane Burton cb. 22 DK Images: Dave King cla, cra; 22 Warren Photographic: Jane Burton tl. 22-23 DK Images: Marc Henrie. 23 DK Images: Dave King tr; Marc Henrie ca. 23 Powerstock: Martin Rugner/age fotostock br. 24 DK Images: Jane Burton cla, clb. 24 OSF/photolibrary.com: cbr. 24 Powerstock: Martin Rugner/age fotostock car. 24 Warren Photographic: Jane Burton cla, car.
All other images © Dorling Kindersley
For further information see: www.dkimages.com